Introduction

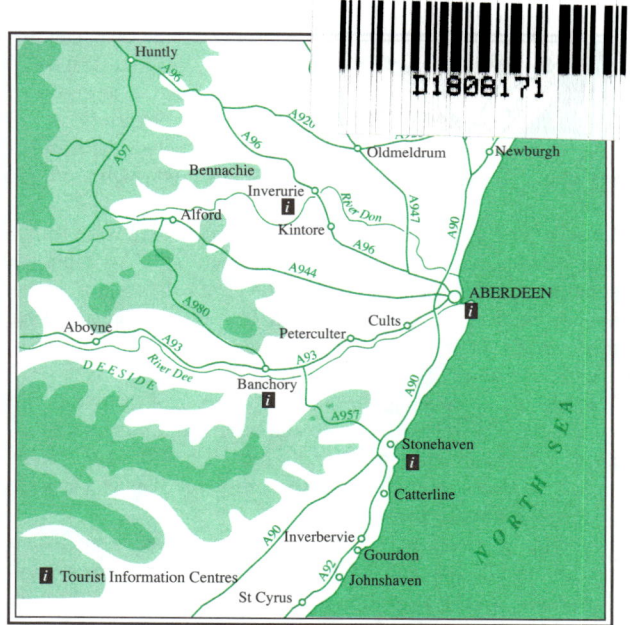

Map labels: Huntly, A96, A920, A96, A97, Oldmeldrum, Newburgh, Bennachie, Inverurie **i**, River Don, A947, A90, Alford, Kintore, A96, A944, A980, ABERDEEN **i**, Aboyne, A93, River Dee, Peterculter, Cults, D E E S I D E, Banchory **i**, A93, A90, A957, Stonehaven **i**, N O R T H   S E A, Catterline, A90, Inverbervie, A92, Gourdon, **i** Tourist Information Centres, St Cyrus, Johnshaven

A t the heart of this area is the city of Aberdeen; sited on the North
Sea coast at the point where the region's two main rivers – the
Don and the Dee – reach the sea. Aberdeen is effectively the capital
of a large area of the north-east of Scotland – the major political,
financial, cultural and educational centre – and is the major service
centre for people far into the Highlands.

Historically, the city was divided into Old Aberdeen and Aberdeen.
The former was centred on the cathedral and the university, at the
mouth of the Don; the latter on the medieval castle, fishing harbour
and port by the River Dee. The two are now joined, but Old Aberdeen
still retains its sense of separateness and a definite Old World charm
(15), while the similarly distinct village of Footdee, at the mouth of

the River Dee, provides a rationalised vision of a traditional fishing settlement *(16)*.

The city's major economic role nowadays is as the main centre for the British North Sea oil industry. Although there are still fishing boats in the harbour, therefore, they are dwarfed by the strangely-shaped tugs and support vessels which service the offshore rigs *(16,18)*, while the area behind the docks is packed with the warehouses and offices of numerous ancillary industries which profit from the boom.

Between the two river mouths stretch the splendid golden sands of Aberdeen Beach, backed by the long Esplanade *(16)* – an improbable yet popular resort, on those days when the grim North Sea weather relents – while over the low hills behind the links are spread the grey granite terraces of 18th- and 19th-century Aberdeen, interspersed by parks and other areas of greenery *(17)*.

The sands continue along the coast to the north of the mouth of the Don: some ten miles (16km) of splendid beaches culminating in the spectacular dunes around the estuary of the River Ythan *(2)*. North of this the sands give way to cliffs which themselves display a spectacular, and more dramatic, beauty *(1)*.

Behind this northern coast is a land of broad horizons, enclosing rolling farmland dotted with small plantations and criss-crossed by minor roads linking small settlements. The largest town in the area is Ellon *(3,12)*, by the River Ythan. For those who particularly enjoy this type of landscape, the Formartine and Buchan Way provides 54 miles of pathway along the bed of the disused railway line linking Fraserburgh and Peterhead in the north with Dyce in the south *(12)*.

North-west of Aberdeen is the hillier farm land around the River Don. The major town on the river is Inverurie – an important agricultural centre at the confluence of the Don and the Urie – and just to the west of that is Bennachie: the site of the best hill walking in the area *(7,8,9,10,11)*. Bennachie is not a single hill, but a long, low, heathery ridge topped by a string of sharp summits and tors – the distinctive horn shape of Mither Tap can be seen for miles around. Around the foot of the hill there is extensive conifer woodland, which provides miles of forest walks, while a long-distance path – the Gordon Way

– heads westwards from the Bennachie Centre *(10)*.

Directly to the west of Aberdeen there is a semi-urban area of mixed dormitory towns, industry and farming. At its worst it is a mess, but if you can rise above it – as at Tyrebagger Hill *(13)* and Elrick Hill *(14)* – there are splendid views over the city to the coast, and over the farmland to the Grampian Mountains to the west. There are also a number of short forest walks which are of particular value to local dog owners *(22)*.

To the south-west of the city is Deeside. This is not the hill-walkers' paradise of Royal Deeside (see *Walks Deeside*), but the gentler, eastern end of the valley. The railway used to run by the river as far as Ballater, and a number of dormitory towns sprang up near the city in the 19th century: Cults, Bieldside, Peterculter. The trains no longer run, but it is still possible to walk along the line back into Aberdeen *(21)*. A further stretch of the line can be walked east of Banchory *(19)* – a busy service centre and the largest town in Deeside – as far as the village of Crathes. Near the village is the splendid Crathes Castle: one of the finest surviving examples of Scots Baronial architecture, and with a wonderful garden. The castle is in the ownership of the National Trust for Scotland and there are a number of walks laid out through the wooded grounds *(20)*.

To the south of Aberdeen the coast is rocky; the high cliffs being pierced only occasionally. The one major town on this stretch of coast is Stonehaven *(22,23)*, behind the narrow bay at the mouth of the Cowie and Carron Waters. South of this the cliffs again take over, providing a spectacular setting for the magnificent ruin of Dunnottar Castle *(23)*. Where the cliffs relent there are occasional towns and villages: Catterline, Inverbervie, Gourdon, Johnshaven *(24)* and St Cyrus *(25)*, with its magnificent sandy beach: a nature reserve.

In addition to Crathes Castle, the area offers short walks round the woodlands of two other splendid National Trust Properties – Drum Castle outside Banchory *(6)*, and Castle Fraser near Kintore *(5)* – as well as the splendid planned gardens at Pitmedden near Oldmedrum *(4)*.

Dunnottar Castle

1 Collieston to Old Slains

A fine cliff-top walk from a small harbour village to a ruined castle, with a return along quiet public roads. Length: **3 miles/5km**; Height Climbed: **150ft/40m**, undulating. ***Please Note: cliff-top walks are dangerous, particularly in high winds. This route is unsuitable for small children and animals if they are not kept under control at all times.***

Collieston is a pretty harbour village – once a fishing village – set in a break in the cliffs north of Forvie Sands (*see* Walk 2). To reach it, drive 10 miles north from the centre of Aberdeen on the A92 road and turn off onto the A975 for Peterhead. After six miles the B9003 cuts off to the right and drops down towards the village. There is no parking in the village itself, so turn left before you reach it into the Cransdale car park. (To walk to the village, follow the path over the little promontory to the south of the car park.)

From the car park, scramble up the rough steps in the cliff leading to the foot of a wooden staircase which climbs steeply to the top of the cliffs. Once there, turn right and follow a rough, grassy path with a field boundary to the left and the cliff-top to the right.

It is a short walk to the ruin of Slains Castle, which is soon visible on its rocky promontory. It is possible to walk down to the ruin, **but keep well clear of the walls in windy weather as the remaining masonry is not secure.**

The castle was the seat of the Hays of Errol until it was sacked in the religious conflicts of 1560, after which they moved to another Slains

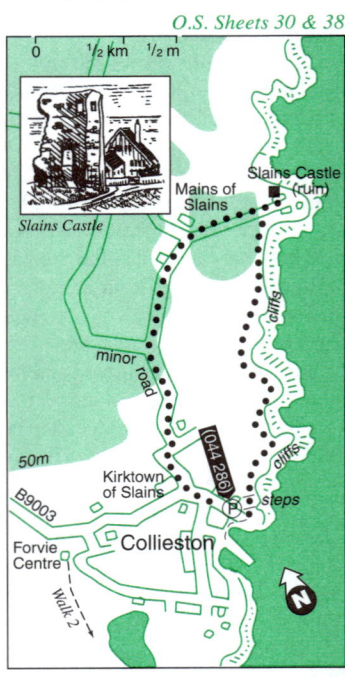

O.S. Sheets 30 & 38

Castle – now also ruined – north of Cruden Bay.

Walk back up the road from the castle. At the junction by Mains of Slains Farm, keep left. Follow this track to the minor public road then turn left again, back to Collieston.

A splendid circuit through sand dunes and along low cliffs, leading to the estuary of the River Ythan. The area is a nature reserve, and will be of particular interest to botanists and ornithologists. Length: up to **8 miles/13km**; *Height Climbed: undulating. Dogs on leads.*

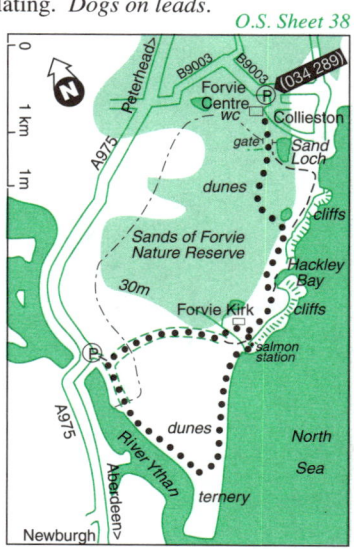

O.S. Sheet 38

To reach the start of this walk, drive 10 miles north of Aberdeen on the A92, then turn onto the A975 road for Peterhead. Follow this for a further six miles then turn right onto the B9003 for Collieston. The entrance to the Nature Reserve is to the right.

Park in the car park and walk on, leaving the information centre to the right. Follow the clear path, signposted for the Nature Reserve, down to a gate. Immediately beyond there is a three-way split. Go straight on. This path is marked by a green arrow. Continue to follow these arrows at subsequent junction as the path winds through splendid, hillocky sand dunes down to join the path running along the top of the cliffs.

For a short circuit, turn left here to return to Collieston (red/green). For the longer walk, however, turn right (red). Follow the path past Hackley Bay. It is possible to explore the sandy beach from the south end, otherwise, continue along the cliff-top to the ruin of Forvie Kirk. Continue beyond this; dropping down to cross a small burn and then continuing to join a large, clear track. Turn right along this (blue/red), following this out of the Nature Reserve and on down to the side of the Ythan Estuary. Turn left at a T-junction and walk on beside the estuary, with splendid views across the mud flats to the right and of the high dunes on the coast ahead.

The path re-enters the Reserve and continues until it reaches the edge of the sands. At this point there is a junction. Go left (blue). The path is metalled at first, then continues, through rolling sand, down to the coast. Follow the beach until, just before it ends, you cross a stream. Turn left, inland (blue), passing an old salmon station. At a junction beyond turn right to return to Forvie Kirk.

A short walk through the parkland and woodland by the side of the River Ythan, where it flows through the small town of Ellon. Paths clear and generally good. Length: **3 miles/5km**; *Height Climbed:* negligible.

O.S. Sheet 30

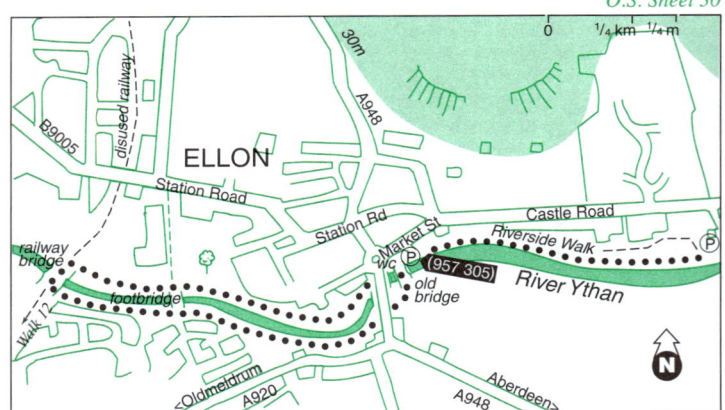

To reach Ellon, drive 15 miles north from the centre of Aberdeen on the A92. Parking is not too difficult in the town, and there is a car park off Market Street, by the river (*see* map).

Walk downstream from the car park into Ythan Court, where there is a sign for the 'Riverside Walk'. The path leads half a mile/1km through pleasant parkland to a further car park at its far end. Return by one of the alternative paths through the park.

From the car park, continue upstream by the riverside; under the two bridges and past the wooden footbridge leading to houses on the other side. Continue on the same side of the river, following a clear path through reeds and flowers, and passing to the left of two overgrown ponds.

The tall railway bridge (which now carries the Formartine & Buchan Way – *see* Walk 12) is visible ahead. As the path approaches it it swings to the right and climbs up the embankment to the old line. Turn left, across the bridge, then drop down to the left, on steps, to join a tarmac track.

Walk back by the riverside; passing under the new road bridge and then turning left across the old stone bridge to return to the start of the walk.

Aberdeenshire has a number of fine old houses and castles, with extensive grounds open to the public. The three described here provide pleasant parkland and woodland walking. (See also Walk 20).

Walk 4) Pitmedden Garden (NTS):
Formal gardens and a woodland walk

Pitmedden is four miles west of Ellon on the A920. Its main feature is a splendid 17th-century-style formal garden, which includes over five miles of box hedges.

There is a waymarked walk through the woodland and parkland surrounding the property. The walk is 1¾ miles/2.8km in length and passes ponds and an old lime kiln.

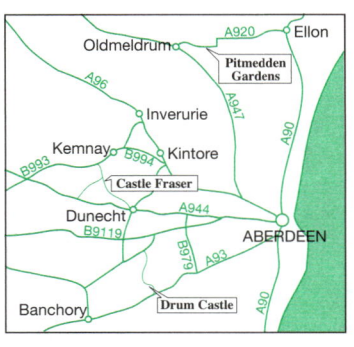

Walk 5) Castle Fraser (NTS):
Castle, gardens and woodland walks

Castle Fraser is one of the grandest of the famous 'Castles of Mar' – elaborate, turreted structures of the 16th/17th century. It is six miles south of Inverurie on minor roads.

The castle is open to the public, along with a walled garden and the extensive grounds. There are two walks laid out through the surrounding woodland and farmland of 1¼ miles/2km and 1½ miles/2.4km.

Walk 6) Drum Castle (NTS):
Castle, gardens and woodland walk

To reach this walk, drive 6 miles east of Banchory on the A93. Look for the National Trust signs for Drum Castle and turn left on the minor road. Follow the signs for the castle and park in the car park.

The castle and formal gardens are open to the public. There is also a pleasant woodland circuit of ¾ mile/1km. To reach this, walk out the top of the car park to reach the gate into the woods.

7 Bennachie A/B/C

Without doubt, the finest area of mixed moor, hill and woodland walking within the area covered by this book. There are four car parks around the hill, with an information centre at the most easterly (see map below), from where a leaflet/map is available. From three of the car parks there are a number of short, waymarked, forest walks (see individual maps), whilst from all four there are signposted routes to the various summits – including Mither Tap, with its splendid Iron Age fort – and across them to the other car parks. In addition, there are clear, low-level paths and tracks linking the three northern car parks.

The map on this page shows the waymarked routes across the hill; the smaller maps opposite show the waymarked circuits from each car park. For two alternative circuits, see the following two pages. For the Gordon Way – a waymarked, lineal route – see Walk 10.

O.S. Sheet 38

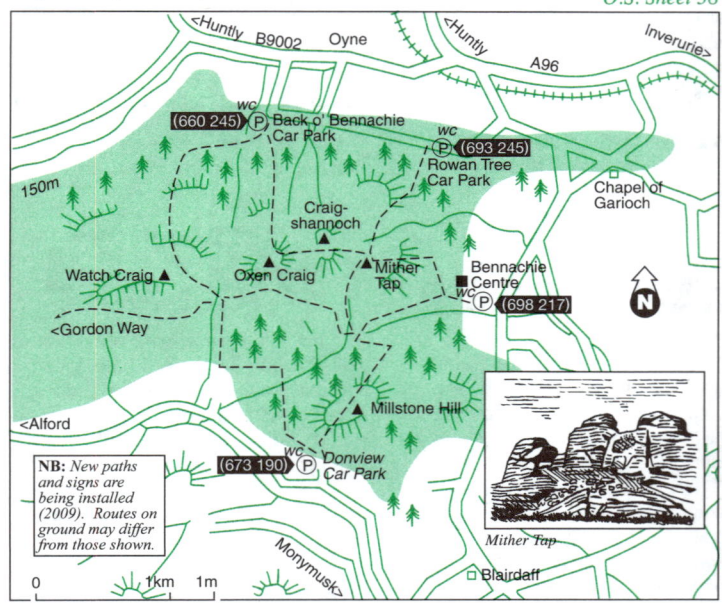

Mither Tap

Bennachie Centre (map 1):
To reach the centre, drive 2 miles north from Inverurie on the A96 for Inverness, then turn left (shortly after joining the by-pass) on the minor road signposted for Chapel of Garioch. Turn left at the junction in the hamlet and continue for a further 2 miles.

There are five waymarked circuits from the car park – from ⅓ mile/0.5km to 3½ miles/5km – the longest a hill walk. (*see also* Walks 8 and 10).

Rowan Tree Car Park:
To reach this car park, follow the instructions as above as far as the junction in Chapel of Garioch, but this time carry straight on. The car park is 1 mile along this road, to the left.

There are no waymarked circuits, but this is the start of the best walk up Mither Tap (*see* Walk 8).

Donview Car Park (map 2):
To reach this car park, drive 3 miles west from Kemnay on the B993 to Monymusk. Turn right, through the village and continue for 1 mile (ignoring roads to the left). After crossing the River Don, take the first turn to the left, then turn left again at the next junction as indicated by the signposts. The car park is a further 2 miles along this road.

There are three waymarked circuits from the car park – from ½ mile/1km to 4¾ miles/7.5km; one a short climb. (*see* Walk 11).

Back o' Bennachie Car Park (map 3):
To reach this car park, drive 7 miles north from Inverurie on the A96 for Inverness, then turn left onto the B9002. Follow this for 1 mile to Oyne,

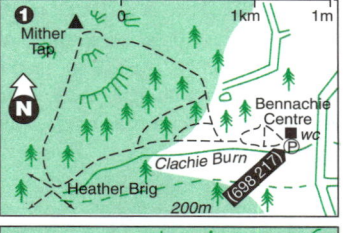

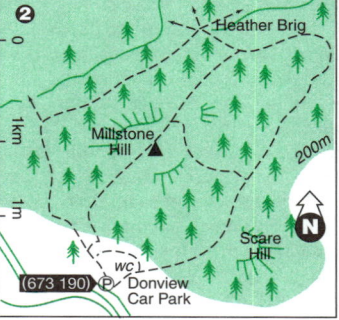

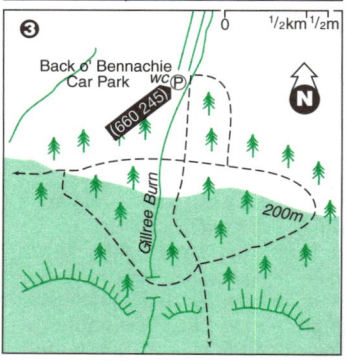

then turn left, just beyond the village.

There are three waymarked circuits through the forest, from ½ mile/1km to 1½ miles/2.5km. (*see* Walk 9).

A fine circuit on clear tracks and rough footpaths; starting through low-lying farmland and woodland, then climbing through conifer woodland and across the open moor to the Iron Age fort on the summit of Mither Tap. Splendid views. Length: **5 miles/8km**; *Height Climbed:* **1200ft/ 360m**.

O.S. Sheet 38

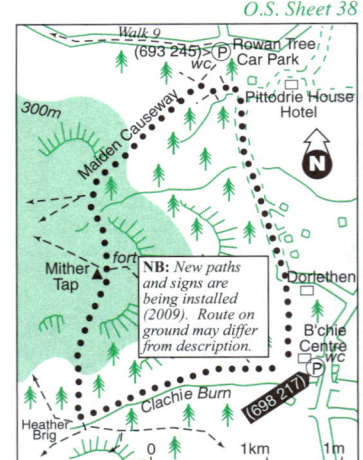

This route starts from the Bennachie Centre. To reach this, follow the directions given in Walk 7.

Look for a sign for 'All Trails'. Do not follow the 'trails' path here; go right, following a path up and across the slope through conifers, to reach a gap in a wall. Beyond this, go right on a clear track running across the slope.

A clear track comes up from the right (Dorlethen) and turns hard right to continue in your current direction. Carry straight on along this, ignoring paths to the right and left, until, almost abreast of the turrets of Pittodrie House Hotel to the right, the path crosses a small burn. Swing left behind a house and then climb up by the burn to a junction.

Keep left, climbing through the trees by the burn. At a four-way junction, go right. After a short distance this path joins the path for Mither Tap from the Rowan Tree car park. Turn left onto this and continue up the slope; emerging onto the open moorland and continuing to climb on the 'Maiden Causeway'. A path cuts off to the right, signposted for Craigshannoch. Ignore this and continue to the splendid Iron Age fort on the summit of Mither Tap.

There is a sign for the car park,

pointing left at a four-way junction, on the near side of the summit. Ignore this: climb to the top then return to the junction and turn left. A clear path marked by green arrows drops down a steep path on the far side of the hill, heading for a pronounced 'V' in the edge of the trees below.

Follow this path down through scattered trees to reach a junction. Keep left, then left again after a further 20m (Gordon Way – GW). This path descends to join a clear forest track. Turn left along this and follow the signs for the Gordon Way back to the Bennachie Centre.

A fine circuit, starting as a climb through woodland and open moorland to the tor at the peak of Oxen Craig (with a possible extension to Mither Tap), then dropping to return along the level track of the Old Aberdeen Turnpike. Length: **5¹/₂ miles/9km** (add **¹/₂ mile/1km** if climbing Mither Tap); Height Climbed: **1250ft/380m**.

O. S. Sheet 38

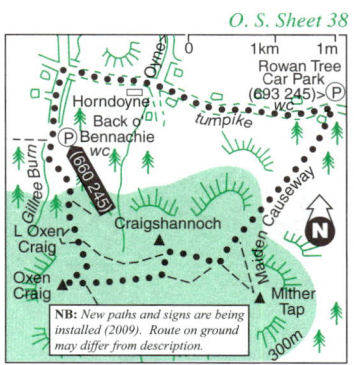

This route starts from the Back o' Bennachie car park. To reach this, follow the directions given in Walk 7.

Walk out the back of the car park and follow signs for all walks up the glen of the Gillree Burn through conifers. A number of short forest walks turn off this route. Ignore these and climb uphill, by the burn, until you exit the trees.

Once you are above the trees an arrow points right, along a clear path. A short distance further on the path splits. The clearer path goes to the left, while the right-hand path makes a detour over Little Oxen Craig. Either will do for this route (*see* map).

The two paths rejoin at a four-way crossroads. The path heading eastwards goes directly to Craigshannoch; the other is signposted for Oxen Craig. For this route, follow the latter up to the splendid viewpoint on the summit ridge, then turn left onto the clear path heading eastwards towards the distinctive peak of Mither Tap.

Ignore a path heading right almost immediately and continue to the lowest point of the path. Just as it begins to climb again, turn left onto a clear path heading straight for Craigshannoch. Follow this to the

peak of the hill and then continue eastwards towards Mither Tap. When this path reaches a junction you have a choice. The path ahead leads up to the summit, from where you can double back along the Maiden Causeway to rejoin the route (*see* map). Otherwise, turn left and follow the clear path down to the Rowan Tree car park.

Turn left from the car park, down a road marked as 'Private Access'. This is the Old Aberdeen Turnpike. Follow it along the face of the hill to the top of a minor road leading up from Oyne. Cross this and continue past the farm beyond (Horndoyne) and then on to join another minor road. Turn left up this to return to the start.

A lineal, waymarked, long-distance route through mixed woodland and across open moorland and farmland. The paths are of varying quality but generally clear. Some navigation is needed in places. The route is divided in two by the B992, but there is no convenient parking place near the crossing. **Length: 12 miles/19km** *(one way);* **Height Climbed: 1000ft/300m** *(east to west), with steep undulations.*   *O.S. Sheets 37 & 38*

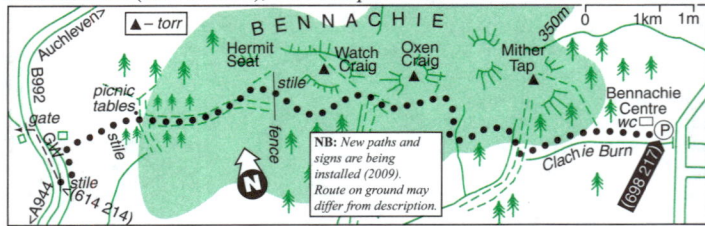

NB: *New paths and signs are being installed (2009). Route on ground may differ from description.*

Eastern Section

This route starts from the Bennachie Centre, on the eastern side of Bennachie. To reach it, follow the directions in Walk 7. A leaflet containing a map of the route is available from the Centre.

From the car park, start walking up the path signposted for 'All Trails'. The early part of the route is clear, following clearly marked forest paths (the insignia on the posts is a stylised 'GW'). After about a mile/1.5km you reach a junction with a forest road. Go left for a short distance (sign: GW), then turn right (GW) on a rough path climbing through trees. Follow this path to a two-part junction in a clearing. Keep straight on at the first junction then go left at the fork just beyond.

The path beyond this point is clear, climbing out of the trees and on to the open moorland. Once on the upper slopes of Bennachie, fine views open up to the west and south. The path aims to the right of Oxen Craig at first, then swings left around a broad swale. Looking ahead, it can be seen contouring around the edge of Oxen Craig and Watch Craig.

Below Oxen Craig there is a junction: keep straight on (GW), along the rougher of the two paths. After a short distance this becomes a clear vehicle track. When this turns hard left go straight on (GW) on a rough footpath through heather.

Below Hermit Seat the path begins to descend and you cross a stile over a fence. A short distance beyond this the path joins a forest track and you turn right. Continue downhill, now through conifers, to reach a T-junction with another forest road. To the right at this point, through a gateway, are some picnic tables in open ground. Ignore these:

go straight across the track ahead and start walking down a very faint, grassy path with a fence to the right.

Follow this down to the end of the trees and cross a stile. Beyond, keep straight ahead (ignoring paths to the left), with a fence to your right. At the foot of the hill turn left, with a small burn to the right, and follow the faint, damp path – overgrown in places – to reach the B992.

Western Section

From the end of the eastern section, turn right along the B992 for a quarter of a mile. Just beyond a white cottage, to the left of the road, there is a gate and a Gordon Way (GW) sign.

Go through the gate and climb up the field beyond, with a fence to the right. Cross a stile at the top and continue, still by the fence. (Priest's Wood becomes visible ahead and to the left. During the following complexities remember that you will ultimately be walking up the side of that wood.)

At the top right-hand corner of this field there is a gate in a deer fence. Go through this and climb the bank beyond to reach a clear, grassy track. Go right along this, with a fence to the right, and continue to reach a T-junction at the point where the fence turns away to the right. Go left (GW) and follow the grassy track – ignoring a path coming in from the left – towards an old farm building. Turn left before reaching the building and drop down, a short distance, to a fence. Turn right along this.

Follow the fence, up the edge of Priest's Wood, to reach a gate in a deer fence on the ridge of Satter Hill. Go through this and drop down the other side (there is no clear path at this point), through scattered larch trees, now with a stone wall to your left.

Beyond the low point you begin to climb again, now with the conifers directly to your left. Watch for a gate to the left. Go through this and you will see a sign for the Gordon Way just beyond. Beyond this a clear, grassy track leads to a junction with a forest road. Go right (GW).

After a short distance there is a further T-junction. Go right again (GW) and follow this forest road for a short way, watching for a Gordon Way sign to the right of the road,

O.S. Sheet 37

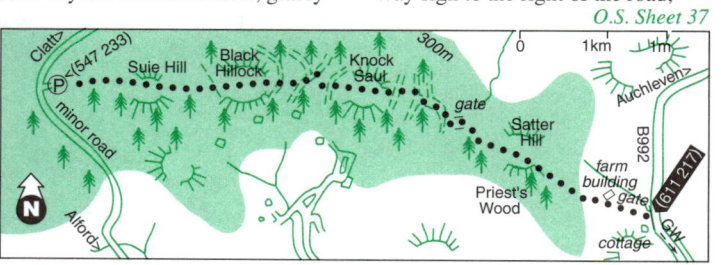

pointing left up a grassy track. Turn on to this.

At the next two junctions keep climbing, straight ahead, and continue up to the open top of Knock Saul, marked by a table and a triangulation point.

Walk straight across and down a ride on the far side. When this reaches a junction with a track go straight across.

Follow the path across a felled area (2008), down a steep slope, to reach a forest road. Go left (GW), then almost immediately left again,

at a junction with another forest road (GW). Follow this road for a short distance to reach a flight of wooden steps to the right.

Climb these and follow the path beyond as it zig-zags up the slope, then continues through conifers to join a forest road. Turn right along this then, almost immediately, left: climbing on a rough path. This quickly swings right. Follow it as it climbs gently to the open top of Suie Hill, then continue beyond, on a clear track, to the car park.

11 **Bennachie: Millstone Hill** _____ B

A waymarked hill climb through conifers leading onto the open top. Paths rough but clear; views terrific. Length: **3¹/₂ miles/5.6km***; Height Climbed:* **1020ft/310m***.*

O.S. Sheet 38

Start this walk from the Donview Car Park (*see* Walk 7). From the back of the car park, follow the red arrows.

The early part of the walk, passing a number of junctions, is difficult to describe but easy to follow – just follow the red arrows. You will eventually find yourself climbing steeply through conifers, then a fringe of birch, before emerging onto the open moorland around the summit. The views from the granite peak – particularly north to Mither Tap – are splendid.

Drop down the far side to reach a junction. Go straight on (ie, the right-hand path) and follow the clear path down into the trees then back, past further junctions, to the car park.

NB: *New paths and signs are being installed (2009). Route on ground may differ from description.*

Millstone Hill

150m

wc

P

Donview Car Park (672 190)

R. Don

N

12 Dyce to Ellon _____ A/B/C

A low-level, lineal route along the bed of a disused railway; passing through an area of mixed farming and occasional woodland. The walk makes use of a section of the longer Formartine and Buchan Way. _Length:_ **13 miles/21km** (one way)_; Height Climbed:_ negligible.

The Formartine and Buchan Way is comprised of some 54 miles/86km of disused railway line, linking Dyce with the fishing ports of Fraserburgh and Peterhead (the two lines split at Maud) to the north-east. The countryside is not dramatic, but there are fine, wide views across rolling countryside.

This walk follows the southern part of this long-distance footpath and can be joined at a number of points. The route is never in doubt.

If starting from Dyce, follow the signs for the station from the centre of the town down Station Road. At the far end of the car park the walk begins on a tarmac path.

From Ellon, the walk can be joined either by following the western half of the Riverside Walk (Walk 3) to the railbridge, or by walking west from the town centre on Station Road and watching for the start of the line to the left.

In addition to Dyce and Ellon, there is parking at Logierieve, Monkshill, Udny Station and Newmachar. Newmachar is given a wide berth and the other villages are small, so you should provision yourself before you start the walk.

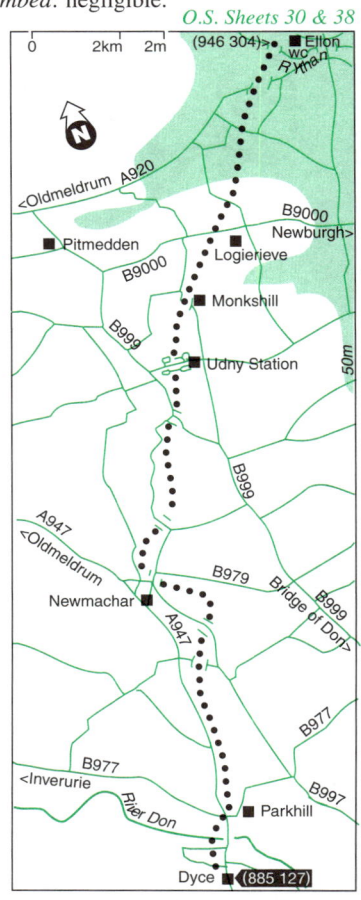

O.S. Sheets 30 & 38

Walks Aberdeen & District

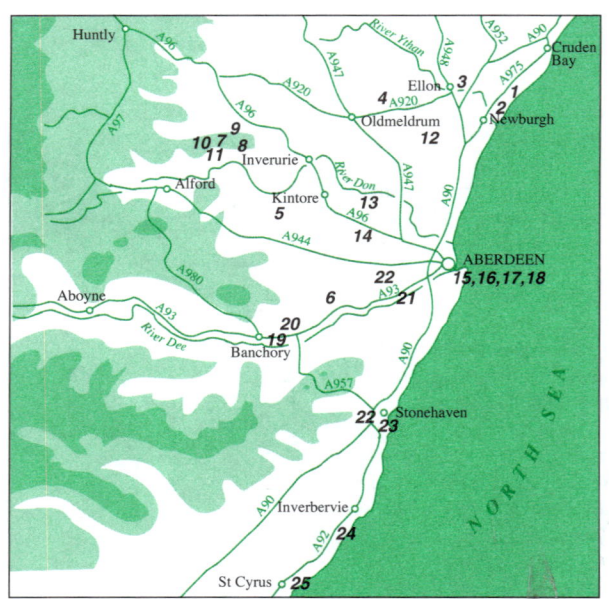

Grades

A ...... Full walking equipment required

B ...... Strong walking footwear and waterproof clothing required

C ...... Comfortable walking footwear recommended

— www.pocketwalks.com —

Published by: Hallewell Publications, The Milton, Foss,
Pitlochry, Perthshire PH16 5NQ
Printed by: Thomson Litho Ltd, East Kilbride

Walks Aberdeen & District

13 **Kirkhill Forest** ⎯⎯⎯⎯⎯⎯⎯⎯⎯⎯⎯⎯⎯⎯⎯⎯⎯ **B**

A short hill climb following a waymarked path through Forest Enterprise woods. Leads to extensive views from a small tower on an open summit. Length: **3¼ miles /5.5km**; *Height Climbed:* **350ft/100m**.

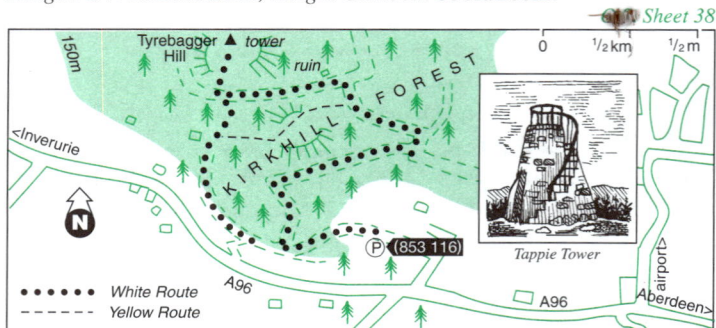

Sheet 38

••••• White Route
– – – – Yellow Route

Tappie Tower

Tyrebagger Hill is a low, forested hill to the west of Aberdeen, just south of the River Don. To reach it, drive six miles from the city centre along the A96 Inverurie road. A short distance after the marked turns for Dyce Airport there is a turn to the right, off the dual carriageway, signposted for Kirkhill Forest. Turn up this road and keep to the left for the car park.

There are two signposted walks through the woods starting from this car park (in addition to the cycle and horse trails and orienteering routes): yellow and white. This route is the walk to the peak of the hill. For this, follow the white waymarkers.

Start on the clear track from the far end of the car park. At a signposted four-way junction, keep straight on (white). Thereafter, stick to the main, clear track through the forest; climbing, swinging right

across the slope, then doubling back uphill to the left to reach a T-junction.

Turn left at this point, back across the slope. Continue until you see a path marked by a white arrow heading off to the left. This is the return route, but before taking it continue for a short distance and then turn right up a clear path, climbing for a short way through the trees to the open top of the hill. Here there is a small stone tower (Tappie Tower) with a flight of steps leading up it. The views from the top are splendid.

Walk back down to the main track to find the start of the return route. This drops down the side of the wood and then swings left, parallel to the road. Continue along this clear track, ignoring paths to right and left, until you rejoin the original track at the first split after the car park.

A modest hill climb through mixed woodland and open grazing land.
Length: **3¹/₂ miles/5.5km**; *Height Climbed:* **260ft/80m**.

O.S. Sheet 38

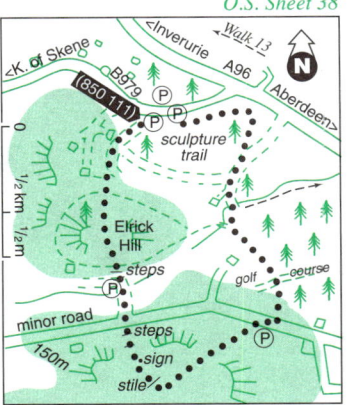

To reach the start, drive six miles
north-west from the centre of
Aberdeen on the A96 road for
Inverurie then turn left, off the dual
carriageway, onto the B979 road for
Kirkton of Skene. A short distance
along this there are three car parks.
Park in the second car park to the left
(Forestry Commission information
board and waymarked walks).

Walk out of the car park on a
clear track which starts near the
information board. At the first
junction go straight on (brown
arrow). Climb up through the trees
then cut right off the track, across a
burn (brown). At the next junction go
left (brown) and climb to a four-way
junction. Go straight on (brown),
climbing through heather to the open
summit of the hill.

Continue straight on beyond,
dropping down to two picnic tables
in a stand of trees. Here there is
a four-way junction: keep straight
on (brown). In a short distance the
path becomes a flight of steps and
drops to a small car park. Climb
up to the road beyond this, then up
the steps directly opposite to reach
a stile. Climb straight on beyond
this, through a band of gorse then
up a grass slope to reach a stile over
a fence. Cross this to enter a field.
On the far side of the field is another
band of gorse. Pass through this to
join a metalled track. Turn left to

reach a car park by the road.

Join the road and turn right. After
a short distance turn left at a sign
(Tyrebagger). Follow a clear path
down the edge of a wood, crossing
an access road then continuing by
the edge of the trees until you reach
a burn. Head right to pass the end of
a footbridge – don't cross; stay to the
right of the burn. At the next junction
keep straight on (Tyrebagger). The
path then crosses a bridge and climbs.
Two tracks come in from behind-left
in quick succession. Keep straight on
at both junctions.

When a signposted path cuts off
to the left of the main track follow it,
swinging left through mature conifer
woodland. This comes down to
run parallel to the road, through the
eastern car park and back to the start.

A fine circuit featuring the splendid woodland by the River Don (part of the Donmouth Local Nature Reserve) and the Cathedral, University and other handsome buildings of the ancient settlement of Old Aberdeen. A route of particular architectural interest. Length: **3 miles/5km**; *Height Climbed:* undulating.

O.S. Sheet 38

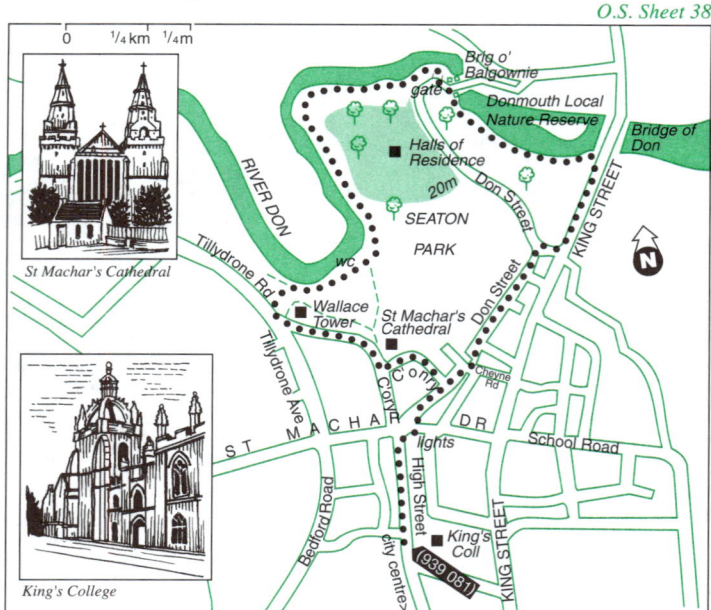

St Machar's Cathedral

King's College

At one time there were two Aberdeens: Old Aberdeen, centred on the Cathedral and University by the River Don, and the fishing and trading port of 'New' Aberdeen – which was a significant settlement itself in medieval times – on the estuary of the River Dee. In 1891 the burgh of Old Aberdeen lost its independence. It retains its own identity, however, and clearly constitutes a separate town centre within the city.

From the centre of the city, a variety of buses link Union Street with Old Aberdeen. Please check with the Tourist Information Centre for details (*see* inside back cover).

Start walking from King's College, a short distance down High Street from its junction with St Machar Drive. This is the heart of Aberdeen University. The tower is part of King's College Chapel: the earliest building in the University, begun in 1500.

Walk down to St Machar Drive and cross at the pedestrian crossing to reach Don Street. Follow Don Street until it is half-blocked ahead and Cheyne Road cuts off to the right. Take the cycle route past the block and carry straight on, ultimately reaching a T-junction. Cross the road ahead, go right for 30m, then turn left at a second T-junction (King Street). Follow this busy road to the near end of the bridge over the River Don.

Just before the bridge there is a sign to the left indicating a path to Brig o' Balgownie. Turn onto this path and follow it through the woods in the narrow valley of the Don beyond, up to join the road at the end of Brig o' Balgownie  – one of the oldest bridges still standing in Britain, with parts dating back to the early 14th century. Turn left, through houses. Beyond the last house turn right through a gate in a wall: the entrance to Seaton Park.

Follow the path beyond through the trees above the river, with the University halls of residence over the fence to the left. The river swings hard left and the path follows it, passing through a fine stand of beech trees and then dropping down to the main part of the park.

Follow the path by the river through the park. At the end of the park a metalled path continues by the river for a short distance, then becomes rougher, pulls away from the river and splits. Go left, climbing to reach a road.

Turn left along this, then immediately left again, following a cobbled lane passing to the right of the distinctive Wallace Tower: a town house built in 1610, which stood in the centre of Aberdeen until it was moved in 1964.

At the bottom of the lane is St Machar's Cathedral. This striking building dates primarily from the 15th century, although it is not the first church to have stood on the site and contains earlier elements. The current building – notable for its simple severity – was originally much larger, but the central tower collapsed in 1688.

By the entrance to the Cathedral grounds the road (now the Chanonry) veers right. At the far end of the grounds turn left down the Chanonry and follow it to the junction with Don Street. Turn right up this to reach St Machar Drive. Turn left along this for a short distance to the crossing point, cross over, then double back and turn left up High Street to return to the start.

Return to the city centre by bus.

A town walk past the docks and buildings of the thriving Aberdeen Harbour, leading down to a charming planned fishing village at the mouth of the River Dee. Possible extension along the Esplanade. Length: **3 miles/5km** (from the centre of Aberdeen, returning either by the same route or via the Esplanade); *Height Climbed:* negligible.

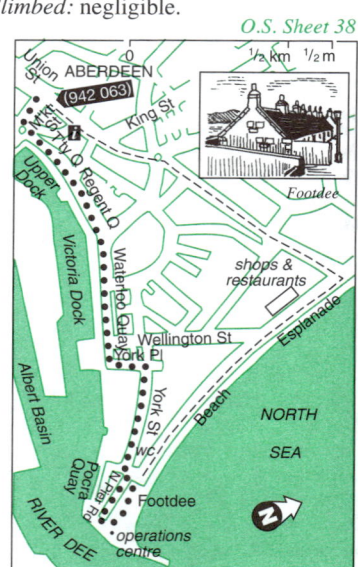

O.S. Sheet 38

Footdee is a village within a city: a small area of terraced houses by the mouth of the River Dee, separated from the rest of Aberdeen by the industrial area around the docks and the broad links behind the Esplanade.

To reach the village, walk south from Union Street down Market Street. When the harbour appears ahead turn left along Trinity Quay, keeping the road to your right with the dock beyond. When the road pulls away from the quay, cross at a set of lights then double back for a short distance before turning left along Regent Quay.

At the end of Regent Quay there is a junction with another road. Keep right and continue along Waterloo Quay. Turn left up York Place, then right along York Street (at the junction marked by the Neptune Bar).

At the end of the street cross the road ahead, jink left and turn right down New Pier Road, with the first houses of Footdee to the left. Continue until you reach the quayside. Turn left, past the Silver Darling Restaurant, to reach the entrance to the Marine Operations Centre. Turn left on the near side of the gate to join a clear path with the sea to your right and the quiet

conservation village to your left.

At the end of the houses, turn left to return to the end of New Pier Road. At this point you can either return by the original route or turn right along the Esplanade, with the sands of Aberdeen Beach to the right.

Follow the shore for a mile/ 1.5km, past a row of restaurants and shops, then turn left at a set of traffic lights up a dual carriageway. Follow this back to the centre of the city.

A short walk around the pleasant parkland of Duthie Park, with its ponds, fountains and monuments, plus the splendid hothouses of the winter gardens. In addition, there is a possible extension along the clear footpath by the side of the River Dee. Length: ½ **mile/1km** (around park) **1½ miles/2.5km** (to Bridge of Dee and back)*; Height Climbed:* negligible.

O.S. Sheet 38

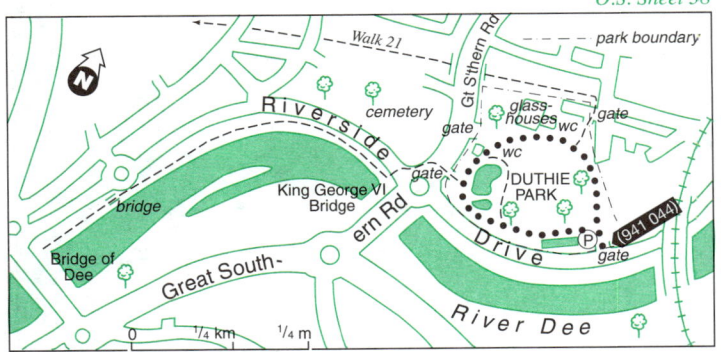

Duthie Park, with its ponds, statues and tree-lined avenues – and, above all, its extensive glass-houses – is the finest park in Aberdeen. Though small (44 acres/18ha), it provides pleasant walking in both summer and winter, and is only a mile/1.5km from the centre of the city.

The park sits in a bend on the north side of the River Dee, just to the east of Great Southern Road, and can be reached from the city centre by turning south down any of the main streets. There are four entrances to the park (*see* map) and a number of paths around it. The distance given above is for a circuit around the edge of the area; obviously, there are alternatives.

If you wish to walk further, there are two options. One is to start walking along the old Deeside railway line (*see* map and Walk 21). A pleasant alternative stroll is to walk up the bank of the River Dee to Bridge of Dee. To do this, leave the park by its western entrance, leading on to Great Southern Road. Cross this at the lights and then turn left, to reach a roundabout. The road cutting right is Riverside Drive. Cross this and drop down to the cinder path running above the river. Follow this for half a mile/1km – crossing an old pack horse bridge along the way – to reach the old bridge over the Dee, parts of which date back to the 16th century.

Return by the same route.

18 **Girdle Ness** B

A circuit on paths and quiet public roads around an exposed headland, returning through a built-up area. Passes Torry Battery viewpoint and a lighthouse, and offers splendid views of Aberdeen Harbour. Length: **3 miles/5km**; *Height Climbed:* undulating.

O.S. Sheet 38

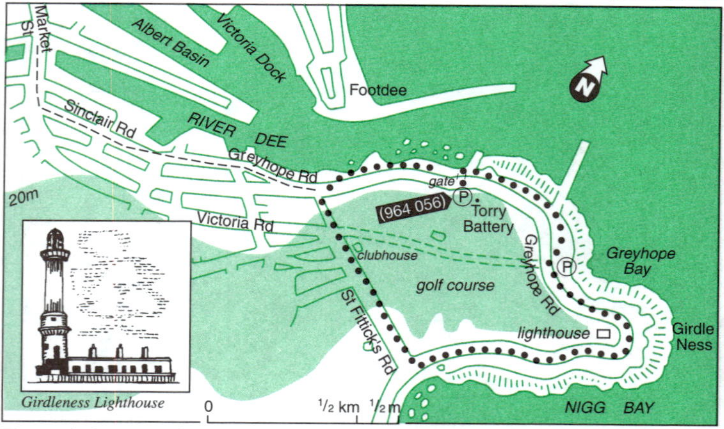

Girdleness Lighthouse

To reach the start of this route, drive (or walk – a distance of two miles/3km) south from Union Street along Market Street – crossing the head of the docks. Cross the bridge over the River Dee and then turn first left onto South Esplanade East. At the T-junction with Sinclair Road turn left. Follow this, and Greyhope Road beyond, through the built-up area south of the river until the buildings end. Watch for a car park up to the right of the road. Already there are splendid views of the docks and the rivermouth.

Leave the car park, cross the road, pass through a gate and follow the path beyond down to the shore. Turn right and continue on or above the shore until, just before the lighthouse on the point is reached, the path joins the road at another car park.

Continue along the pavement; past the lighthouse and on, with a view of Nigg Bay opening up to the left. When the road reaches a junction, just by the head of the bay, turn right; following St Fittick's Road over the neck of the promontory. This passes through a built up area and reaches a junction. Keep straight on, dropping back down to rejoin Greyhope Road.

Turn right. After a short distance a path starts to the left, continuing by the shore back to the start of the walk.

A flat, lineal route along the line of the old Deeside railway, leading through woodland, farmland and urban areas into the centre of Aberdeen. Length: up to **7 miles/11km**; *Height Climbed:* none.

O.S. Sheet 38

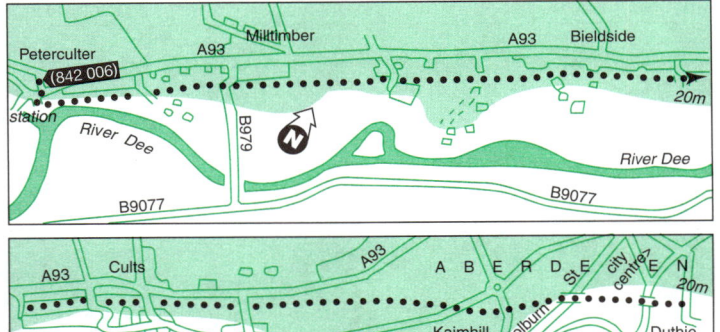

Peterculter is a dormitory town on the north bank of the River Dee, 8 miles west of the centre of Aberdeen on the A93 road for Braemar. It was once a stop on the Deeside Railway. That was closed in the 1960s, but the line of the railway remains and provides a pleasant, flat walk through the towns and farmland of lower Deeside into the city centre.

The route can be walked either way, and presents no navigational difficulties. If starting from Peterculter, look for Peterculter Parish Church on the north side of the main road in the centre of the town. Cross the road and walk down Station Brae almost opposite. When this joins Station Road continue downhill to the site of the old station.

Turn left and walk along the clear track (also ideal for cyclists); passing Milltimber, Bieldside and Cults before entering the outskirts of Aberdeen.

This last section is the least scenic; nevertheless, a couple of handsome new bridges (replacing demolished rail bridges crossing roads) make it possible to continue along the line as far as the entrance to Duthie Park (Walk 17). Alternatively, drop down onto Holburn Street and turn left along it, following it up to the west end of Union Street in the centre of the city.

Three mixed woods owned by the Forestry Commission containing short waymarked walks, a little to the west of Aberdeen, plus an area of mixed woodland on the outskirts of Stonehaven. Length/Height Climbed: see individual entries.

O.S. Sheet 38

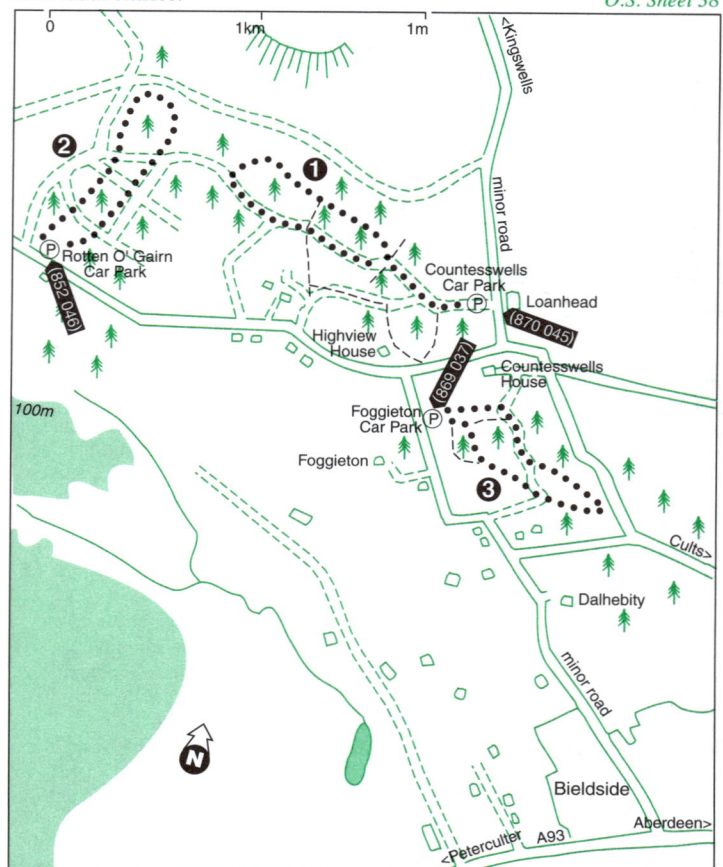

1 Countesswells:

To reach the car park, drive west from Aberdeen on the A93 road for Braemar. When the road reaches Cults (three miles from the city centre) turn right (north) at the traffic lights onto a minor road. Beyond the town there is an unmarked V-junction. Keep right. At the next two junctions follow the signs for Kingswells. The car park is to the left, just beyond the second.

Three signposted routes through conifer and mixed woodland. *Length:* Red **1 mile/1.5km**; Yellow **1¼ miles/2km**; Green **1½ miles/2.5km**; *Height Climbed:* negligible.

2 Rotten O' Gairn:

Directions as above as far as Cults. Then drive on along the A93 for a further mile to Bieldside and turn right on the minor road signposted for Blackford. Follow this road to a T-junction and turn left. The car park is a mile further on to the right.

One walk through mixed woodland. Some climbing involved. *Length:* **1¼ miles/2km**; *Height Climbed:* **160ft/50m**.

3 Foggieton:

Directions as above, but the car park is to the right of the road about a mile north of Bieldside; a short distance before the T-junction.

Three routes through conifer and mixed woodland. *Length:* Blue, **½ mile/1km**, Yellow, **¾ mile/1km**, Red, **1¼ mile/2km**; *Height Climbed:* negligible.

4 Dunnottar Woodland Park:

Drive south from the centre of Stonehaven on the A957 road. Continue until, just before the junction with the A92, a minor road cuts off to the right. There is no mention of the walks, so watch carefully for the turn. The car park, signposted 'Dunnottar Woodland Park', is almost immediately on your right. A map in the car park shows the paths.

There are a number of possible routes, connected by signposts and passing various points of interest, leading you through the mixed woodland around the glen of a small burn (*see* map). The wood is cut in two by a minor public road. Please note that you can cross this and continue walking beyond. *Length:* up to **2 miles/3km**; *Height Climbed:* up to **100ft/30m**.

O.S. Sheet 45

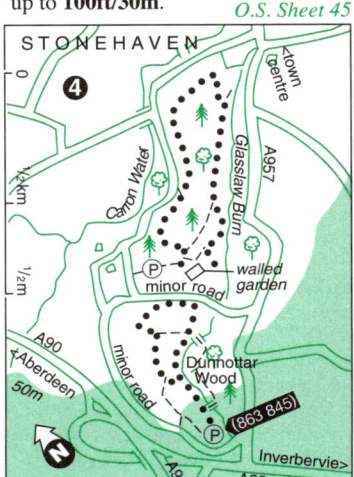

A spectacular circuit through farmland and along cliff tops, passing the ruins of Dunnottar Castle. Return along a quiet public road. Length: 2½ miles/4km; Height Climbed: 200ft/60m, undulating. NB: cliff-top walk: unsuitable for small children and animals if not kept under control. The route description begins at the castle car park: if you are not visiting the castle itself, please start from Stonehaven (see map).

Dunnottar Castle is a magnificent ruin in a dramatic cliff-top position a short distance south of the harbour town of Stonehaven. The site – on a high promontory, separated from the rest of the cliff by a deep declivity – has been used as a defensive site from earliest times, but the oldest remaining section dates from the 14th century. From that time until 1715 the castle was developed by the Earls Marischal (the Keith family) until it was forfeited, following the '15 uprising, and dismantled.

To reach the castle, drive south from the centre of Stonehaven on the A957. Follow this to the junction with the A92. Turn left for 1 mile, then turn left again onto a minor road signposted for Dunnottar Castle. After a short distance there is a small car park to the right.

Follow the track down to the top of the steps leading down into the dip before the castle. Carry straight on to visit the castle. Otherwise, turn left and follow a clear footpath which starts along the cliff top – there is no doubt about the route. As you proceed you will notice the dramatic war memorial on a hill ahead. It is possible to visit this – the entrance is at the far end of the enclosure.

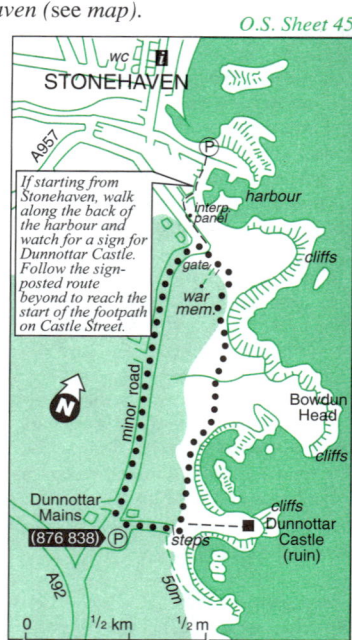

O.S. Sheet 45

If starting from Stonehaven, walk along the back of the harbour and watch for a sign for Dunnottar Castle. Follow the sign-posted route beyond to reach the start of the footpath on Castle Street.

Beyond the war memorial the path joins a minor road. To return to the Dunnottar car park turn left. To reach Stonehaven, turn right for a short distance, watching for the start of a footpath to the right by an interpretive panel. Follow this path down to the harbour.

A flat, low-level, lineal route along the coast linking three old fishing villages, two with harbours. Length: **4 miles/6.5km** *(one way); Height Climbed:* negligible. *There is a possible alternative return by the local bus service. Check times locally.*

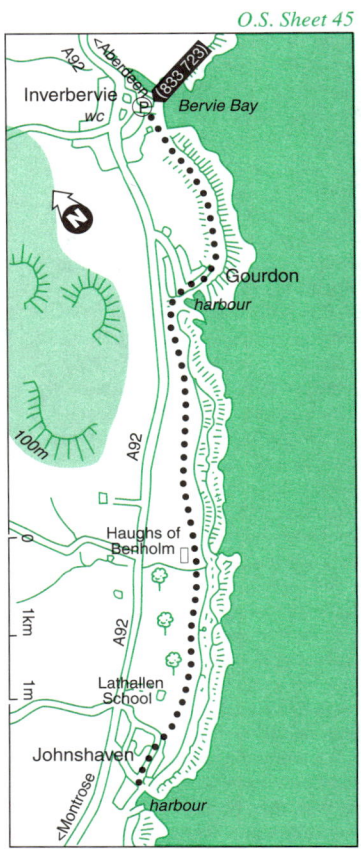

O.S. Sheet 45

The town of Inverbervie lies on the coast, 9 miles south of Stonehaven on the A92. To reach the start of this route, turn off Inverbervie main street at the sign for the caravan park (ie, down Kirkburn). Follow this road down to a car park behind the beach.

Inverbervie has no harbour; nevertheless, the town does have one strong link with Britain's maritime heritage: it was the birthplace of Hercules Linton, the designer of the famous tea clipper *Cutty Sark*.

Start walking south from the car park along a vehicle track. As you leave the houses cut left to join a path running along the flat ground behind the shingle shore. It is only one mile/1.5km to the old fishing port of Gourdon. Follow the road through the village to reach the harbour. Beyond this, follow the sign for the 'Off-road Cycle Route': a clear track which starts as a road to the right of the whitewashed Harbour Bar.

Follow this track for three miles/5km along the coast to reach the harbour of the old fishing port of Johnshaven. From here, either return by the same route or catch one of the regular buses back up to Inverbervie.

25 St Cyrus ———————————————— C

A circular walk along the spectacular sandy beach of St Cyrus National Nature Reserve. Short section of cliff-top walking. Length: 3¹/2 miles/5.5km; Height Climbed: 200ft/60m.

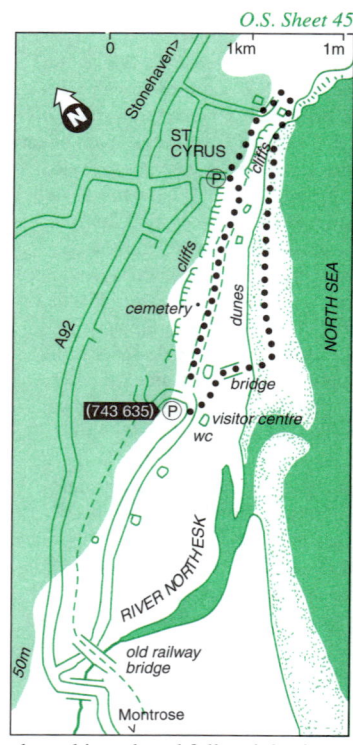

O.S. Sheet 45

The village of St Cyrus is 16 miles south of Stonehaven on the A92. It is possible to start this walk from the village. For the easiest parking, however, continue a further 2 miles south of the village, until, just before the main road swings left to cross the North Esk, a single-track road cuts off sharp left, signposted 'Beach'. Follow this for just over a mile to reach the car park and visitor centre (open May to September).

Cross the road by the car park and follow the signs for the Nature Reserve. The path crosses a long bridge over a marshy area then runs through dunes to reach the beach. Turn left along the sands, walking towards a cottage with a white gable visible on the cliff-top in the distance. (NB: in certain tide and weather conditions you will need to walk behind the dunes).

When you reach the cliffs below the cottage, follow the steep path up to the top of the cliff. Turn left along a tarred path between two houses, then left again along the grassy cliff-top path. There are superb views from this section south towards Montrose and Montrose Basin.

Follow the path as far as a small car park then turn left down a steep path (take care) which leads back down to join a clear path near an old salmon fishing station. Turn right along this path and follow it back to the car park. Along the way you pass the old Nether Kirkyard. Although most of the tombstones have been badly worn by the elements, some still carry very interesting markings and inscriptions.